I NEVER WANTED TO BE GAY... *(BUT DOES ANYONE?)*

by Al Walz

RoseDog Books
PITTSBURGH, PENNSYLVANIA 15238

The contents of this work, including, but not limited to, the accuracy of events, people, and places depicted; opinions expressed; permission to use previously published materials included; and any advice given or actions advocated are solely the responsibility of the author, who assumes all liability for said work and indemnifies the publisher against any claims stemming from publication of the work.

RoseDog Books
585 Alpha Drive, Suite 103
Pittsburgh, PA 15238
Visit our website at www.rosedogbookstore.com

ISBN: 979-8-89027-310-9
eISBN: 979-8-89027-808-1

Be real
Be visual
Be social
Be cynical
Be original
Be suicidal
Be political
Be individual
Be abnormal
Be homosexual
Be controversial
Be unconventional
Be confrontational

Be. AI
An internal, personal & emotional journal

I NEVER WANTED TO BE GAY...

"That is my truth. I mean, why would anyone want to be? Isn't life hard enough already, without having to add in the fact that you're a minority and attracted to the same sex?"

We've been taught that life coexists between men and women, and in order for it to continue, procreation must happen through these two sexes. We're taught to learn throughout our formative years (K- grade 12), to graduate, get a secondary education (in four more years), graduate again, get a professional job, get married, and have children. That was the "structure" of life implanted in me. Nowhere in there did it say anything about falling in love with another man, and creating a life of your own, whatever that may be?

I've spent a good 10 years +, fighting and struggling against this, trying to come to some sort of conclusion of how the "others" (homosexuals, minorities, and those who don't fit the "white middle class" mold of historical American society) are "supposed" to live, and what our structure is "supposed" to be like, and am slowly, finally, figuring it all out.

After infinitely endless hours of therapy, reading self-help books, thousands of nights spent crying, pretending to be someone else, and moving around from job to job, city to city, I think I have come up with a conclusion. It doesn't matter. It doesn't matter if you're gay, straight, black, white, rich, poor - we're all here doing the best we can. And we're only going to be here for what is actually a "blink in time" in history, so why not live your truth, whatever that may be? Why spend so many days, nights, weeks, months, and years "pretending" to be something that you know doesn't really fit into your "grand scheme of things", but yet, this is what you think you are supposed to do, because no one has shown/taught you otherwise? Whether it be living "in the closet", pretending to be butch when you're really femme (and vice-versa), getting married and having kids (even though you're not really sure you want them - you just feel like you're "supposed to"), or working a "corporate", nine-to-five, forty-plus hours a week job, for so many years, to then realize you've done nothing else but that.

Even though we are "taught" a generalized "structure" of living, doesn't mean we really have to follow it. Won't it mean much more to us in the long run, knowing we followed our hearts and truths and broke away from that structure, as hard as it may be, but now living our lives on our own terms? This is something I know I would like, and pretty much what I have done, and continue to do so, which is the topic for this essay - living on your own terms, following your bliss, exploring your passions and doing them. Whatever it may sound like to you, it's all good. It's <u>your life</u> and you only get one chance to live it. What's stopping you?

I understand. I've been there. I know what slowed me down in never fully thinking that I could do that; that I was allowed to, but I'm here to tell you that it's ok, and it's never too late to start. At 53, I'm ready to "take charge of my life" and stop living like I'm programmed to think that this is how I'm supposed to live. And this is my story...

*I AM **AL** (ONE)*

With my thoughts, in my head,
With my books, in my bed,
With my music, in my car,
At a club, at a bar.
With my dinner, in my house,
Silent stirring, as a mouse.
With Red Vines, at the movies,
Or outside, among the trees.
On my bike, at the gym,
Next to her, next to him,
When I meditate, it is wanted,
Aggravated, I am haunted.
When I'm on line, I am hidden,
Crying out seems forbidden?
So I'll post something happy,
And pretend all is good.
While inside I feel crappy,
And most misunderstood.
Another day arrives, awaken by myself,
Continues to erase my state of mental health,
As my loneliness will keep spreading,
Day will end; night I'll be dreading.

ORIGIN <u>AL</u>

He was born in the east,
Then he headed out west,
To find a happier, brighter life;
To make a new home, his nest.

He packed up his Geo Metro,
Said good-bye to his mom.
It was time to let go,
From his childhood, that was gone.

For four days he had driven
Through dry lands and some snow.
As each day brought him closer
To something, he did not know.

California, he had made it,
Pennsylvania, now gone.
San Francisco held beginnings;
A new day comes, new dawn.

What would now happen here?
Will it ever really show?
Only that was determined,
By how much he would grow.

He had low confidence,
Yet he came, anyway,
Knew this place he had landed
Would accept him as gay.

Got a job in the Castro,
And a home right there, too.
Built a life with a boyfriend
Seems like that's what you do?

But like most things, it ended,
Was a sad, teary day.
Packed up once more and headed
For down south, to LA.

Childhood dreams, finally granted,
Fame, celebrities, Hollywood.
Did this actually happen?
Could this be his new "hood"?

So for ten years he "struggled",
Tried to make a new start.
One that had finally suited him;
One to show off his art.

Different places, different spaces,
A new roommate, new job.
Not much closer to being happy
"Is this it?", he would sob.

Though he moved far away,
He still felt all the same.
Finally figured it out;
He'd been playing the wrong game.

So he worked on himself -
Meditation, therapy.
Antidepressants, read self-help books;
Even drank "magic" tea.

Some had helped, just a little;
Still he had a ways to go.
Spent a year unemployed,
Thinking time had moved slow.

In the interim, found a boyfriend,
That was wise beyond his years.
Helped encourage, support, and love him;
Tried to mop up Al's tears.

But decided he should move again -
It was all that he knew.
Hoped his boyfriend would come with him;
To the desert, they flew.

Maybe Palm Springs would suit them;
Only time would help know.
Change is always there for you -
Take advantage, and grow.

No one knows where their headed,
But we face each day strong.
I can't tell you what happens;
Just we don't live, very long.

As for Al and his partner,
They both took a "leap of faith".
We won't know how it turns out;
Good things come to those who wait.

Life's a crapshoot, take a chance.
Just keep moving, as you dance.
You only get once – so try now.
Doesn't matter what, where, why, or how.

Even those with no purpose,
So it seems as we live.
Maybe we're meant to just love and teach,
And that's all that we give.

EXPECTATIONS

I expect everyone to act just like me.

The things that they do – the way they should be.

Be courteous, kind - aware of your way,

Say, "please" and "thanks" always, and "have a nice day!"

The only thing is, which makes me quite sad,

I push away everyone, who makes me quite mad.

I get so frustrated when others don't think,

Which causes me sometimes to create a big stink.

I wonder sometimes, why I'm always alone;

It's because I'm this way, and have not really grown.

I'm not sure I can blame anything on how I've become.

I thought we were all supposed to be perfect employees, boy-
friends, and son.

I felt a little bit small when I found out I'm gay,

And kept secretly hoping, that it might go away.

I didn't think I would ever be looked at, as special,

I felt I needed to create a perfect mind, soul, and vessel.

You would think that I'd lost issues, long time ago,

But I'm fifty-three now, and I still need to grow.

I still feel very small, and though in a big city,

My life still seems really petty, and lately, real shitty.

I still put a ton of expectations on everyone else,

Most the time, these are mainly just placed on myself.

So I try to relax, and to let it all go,

But I guess it's not my role that I play in this show.

It's a sickness, a madness, a disease I can't grasp.

Didn't think it would go on this long, it would last.

But I guess I've no choice – I'll keep taking my meds,

And if you ever encounter me, please forgive what I've said.

TOO MANY UNANSWERED QUESTIONS

I am a waste of life,
Who's taking up space,
As I'm sitting around,
Always feeding my face.

I'm getting real stoned,
While I sit here alone,
Working a dead-end job,
In a shack of a home.

Is this all that I'm for?
Can this really be it?
I would rather be dead,
Than to deal with this shit!

So what's it all about?
This thing we call life?
Are we supposed to buy a house?
Are we supposed to have a wife?

Are we supposed to wear a suit to work?
And to have our weekends off?
Are we supposed to bear children who never obey?
Are we supposed to make more than $50 a day?

It's all about being happy,
And doing whatever you like.
So what if you're having an affair?
So what if your wife's a dyke?

So what if your son might dress up in drag sometime?
So what if your husband never comes home on time?
So what if your daughter gets pregnant – oh no!
So what if your wife leaves you – where will you go?

So your life isn't perfect?
Well, nobody's ever is,
But you're true to yourself
And you mind your own biz.

So your life isn't perfect?
Well, nobody's ever is,
Like the end of this poem
It don't matter if it don't rhyme.

WHAT ARE YOU DOING NOW?

What are you doing now?
You were born in a small town in northwestern Pennsylvania.

What are you doing now?
You were raised in a middle-class, Presbyterian family, who attended church every Sunday.

What are you doing now?
You graduated with honors from high school, and only missed a ½ day, in all four years.

What are you doing now?
You attended college at a major university, and graduated with a degree in Advertising

What are you doing now?
You got high, swallowed mushrooms, dropped acid, snorted coke, and took ecstasy.

What are you doing now?
You moved away to Florida to quote "start your career".

What are you doing now?
You waited tables and worked at big theme parks, as a seasonal employee.

What are you doing now?
You led an undercover life, as a homosexual.

What are you doing now?
You slept with anyone who approached you, and took part in numerous group sex encounters.

What are you doing now?
You're just living your life.

What are you doing now?
<u>Not a fucking thing!</u>

AN __AL__ YSIS

I will never relax -
I am WAY too uptight.
Always thought this was wrong,
But it feels, oh so right.

I will worry A LOT!
I will barely get sleep
If I like it or not,
I will sow, what I reap.

I will always play safe
Never stray, far away.
It seems that I'll always be,
Standing right in my way!

I will let myself down.
I suppose others, too.
Sometimes easier to drown,
Than to push – see it through.

But I'm always on time.
Never once I've been late.
You can't say that I'm not,
From the start, at the gate.

I will never get angry,
I will never get sad.
Never share my emotions,
Learned along, that was bad.

But I'm prompt and efficient,
All employers will say
"Always does what he's told to."
Taught how to live this way.

When it comes to myself,
As to what that I want.
I don't feel I deserve it,
Seems I'm better, nonchalant.

I'll continue getting by,
Can't imagine, I'm alone.
Sometimes, easier not to try,
Than to reach for the throne.

I NEVER WANTED TO BE GAY...PT. 2

First off, I should tell you that it's always been in my genes to "people please", which some people refer to as a "people pleaser". Some others might consider that to mean "pushover", "coward", "wimp", or "passive" - someone who puts their life on hold, so that others can live theirs. The two people I've always wanted to please the most are the same two that brought me into this world - Mom and Dad. I always saw their "people pleaser" attributes, and as hereditary dictates, we tend to become the people that raised us, taught us, installed our values/beliefs, and gave us our base structure, in order to act/react to what would/would not be in store for us, in our future.

So, as two heterosexual people, who grew up in white, middle-class, non-divorced families, during the depression, in rural Pennsylvania, they bestowed upon me the best values and knowledge of what they knew and learned from their parents before them. And, I might add, did a great job!

But, as two heterosexual parents, coming from a time when homosexuality was still not discussed "out in the open", they did not know, or probably even imagine, that their youngest child of four would turn out to be, in fact, a gay man, or a homosexual, himself. So they wouldn't know how or what, by learning from their past experiences and lives, to teach a homosexual about what he was supposed to do. They would only be able to share with him what they knew and experienced themselves. So, that is what I was taught. I was raised, as I'm sure most are raised, to believe that I would, too, one day, probably get married, have a professional career, and eventually have kids.

Well, obviously that wasn't going to work for me, knowing what I knew back then. I knew somehow I was different. I didn't want to admit I was gay, because I didn't want anyone to think I was one of "those gay men" that "everybody" has a vision of in their minds, but no one ever encountered (at least in my town). You know the kind, with the lisp, limp wrist, and outrageously flamboyant feminine gestures. I knew I was not like that, but I also knew that I was probably gay, and would never be able to come out, at least, as long as I was living in North East.

North East, Pennsylvania - a small town in northwest (?) PA, outside of Erie, on the lake, in the farthest northeastern tip of the "thing" that juts out of the state border (before NY), on the left hand side - hence the name. We were a town of about 10,000 (when I was living there) - quaint, quaint, QUAINT - beautiful summers (right on Lake Erie), hazardous winters (right on Lake Erie), and the "perfect" place to raise your children.

RED STATE, BLUE STATE

Red State, Blue State;
We love – you hate.
Is this our fate?
Are we too late?

Whether an elephant, or whether an ass,
Can't we still walk upon each other's grass?
Why is one right? Why is one wrong?
The point is: "Can't we all just get along?"

We're all here; we're each trying, the best that we can,
So why make it harder, for some - each woman and man?
I live my life, gratefully, for me, not you.
How in the world does that really affect you?

Just because we have different views from one another,
Doesn't mean that we're really any better than each other.
What are we gaining, if we can't marry queer?
We're still living beside you – still legally here.

You can have your beliefs; you can still have your fights,
But don't deny us what's ours – don't deny equal rights.
I know we're all entitled to our own opinion,
So keep that. That is yours, but don't make me your minion.

I guess what I'm saying to be perfectly clear,
Is that life's hard already, without adding in fear.
I will respect you and not get in your face,
If you can respect me, and my personal space.

AND/OR?

Should I move,
Or do I stay?
Look for work,
Or play, today?
Am I an artist,
Or a Buddhist?
An Idealist,
Or a nudist?
Maybe a singer,
Or a writer?
A passive soul,
Or a fighter?
How do I choose?
Or will I lose?
Would be so nice
In other's shoes.
I've hit a wall,
And now I crawl.
Out on this ledge,
Afraid I'll fall.
I've wandered this far -
Is this the end?
Or are new beginnings,
Around the bend?
It seems like a waste,
To just disappear.

It's time to turn now,
Away from this fear.
So, do I move,
Or do I stay?
Or wait to know,
Another day?
We're given a lot,
So many great choices.
It's pretty hard to listen,
To all of these voices.
But does it matter?
Will others know?
Whether, if I did,
Or did not grow?
I'm still the same;
I haven't changed.
Just unemployed,
And "rearranged"?
But friends still care,
And family's there.
The love exists –
It's everywhere.
It's not important.
You're still alive.
You have your health -
Forget your pride.
You hit a bump,
As we all do.
That's all it is -
<u>You're still all you!</u>

You're good enough,
As what you are.
Remember this,
And you'll go far.
OR, live in fear,
And disbelief.
You won't escape
Your pain and grief.
Just love your self -
It's all you need
To do right now,
<u>And you'll succeed!</u>

SURVIV__AL__

It's what we're meant to do.
Drink water every day.
Eat healthy, move your feet,
To chase your fears away.

Earn wages - make a living,
So you can pay for things.
Remember - do some giving.
Much happiness it brings.

Get caught up on your sleep,
And smile, often, each day.
When sad, you can still weep,
If skies turn dark and gray.

So, surround yourself with love.
Don't forget to laugh a lot.
Death will always give a shove.
Just enjoy the time you got.

It's ok when times are down.
That's a part of human being.
Better moments come around,
To remind us what we're seeing.

Hold out for one more day.
Tomorrow is a mystery.
Something fortunate might pay,
And realign your history.

Life goes by so very quickly.
Why not struggle through to see?
All which happens , and just could be,
For yourself, friends, family.

You were put here for a reason.
Love created you this way.
Like the changing of a season,
We morph, remold ourselves, as clay.

It doesn't mean it's wrong.
It's just the way <u>YOU</u> are.
The lyrics of <u>YOUR</u> song,
Are yours, to take you far.

Keep singing your own tune.
How you know to stay alive.
Afterlife will come too soon.
Just keep going, and survive.

FEARS

They keep you up at night,
They freeze you, so you stay,
They maximize your fright,
They'll make you lose your way.

They tell you you're no good.
They teach you you're not mad.
They'll overtake your soul,
You'll say, "I'm good", not sad.

You'll never take a risk,
You'll always think you'll fail.
You'll wake up one day pissed.
You crushed your "fairy tale".

They keep you on the ground.
Don't dream too high, you'll fall.
Keep silent, make no sound.
Think big - "No Way!" - stay small.

Meander through your life.
Keep up, it's passing by.
You've got your job, your wife,
Too bad you want a guy.

They keep you safe and "sane",
They keep you off the streets.
You'll soon resist all pain.
You'll soon resist all sweets.

They'll make you doubt yourself.
They'll make you run away.
They'll stay up on your shelf,
Your dreams are safe that way.

That idea will never fly.
"That's stupid, there's no way!"
Just keep on getting by,
You'll get your chance, one day...

You'll wake up, 53,
"What happened? Where'd it go?"
There's so much more to do.
"What do I have to show?"

They'll stop you in your tracks.
You'll say, "I'm happy enough".
You'll slip through all the cracks,
Surrounded by your "stuff".

"As soon as" becomes your motto,
"If only" takes hold of you.
You pray you'll win the lotto,
Show you then, just what I'll do.

But years go by,
You're getting old.
Too late to try,
Is what you're told.

They've won again.
They've beaten you.
They've held you back,
From being you.

EXISTENTI <u>AL</u>

Why are we all here?
Why was I born queer?
What's life all about?
Should I've really come out?

What does become of us?
What's with all of this fuss?
Why are some things best unsaid?
What's it matter, if we're dead?

Why are some driven to succeed?
While others lie in dire need?
Why is there war? Why is there pain?
And what do we really ever, stand to gain?

Why do we hate and why do we fight?
How does it really prove that you're right?
How come some make millions, yearly?
While others get by, maybe, nearly?

Are we born on here to work?
For a promotion, raise, or perk?
What's the point if it could just end?
Our fate may just be 'round the bend.

So we'll never get to spend our money.
And would that be real sad, or real funny?
It makes no sense, our existence.
While our fellow man starves, off out in the distance.

Do you think their envious of all of our greed?
Or just so grateful, to have what they need?
Wonder how it would be if we all lived,
Our life was only just meant to give?

Shelter, food, clothes, and course water,
Enough for mom, dad, son, and daughter.
But yet we seem to just want more
Bigger, faster, toys galore.

Is it a contest? Is that it?
Who really cares if you've got all that shit?
We're at a point where we don't speak
We email, text, blog, and tweet.

Where do you think we'll be in a year?
Maybe none of us will be here?

I NEVER WANTED TO BE GAY...PT. 3

My upbringing was very "stepford-like" in a manner that we (my siblings and I) grew up in a quiet neighborhood, on a quiet street, where we walked to school, played with the kids up the street, kept our houses unlocked and our doors open, for a neighborly visit, night or day. I grew up in a middle-to-upper class family, in a five-bedroom, two-story, two-car garage house. Our family was moderately religious - Presbyterian - church every Sunday, and all children "joined" the church. Both parents were working professionals, and heavily involved in many other extracurricular activities in the community.

I'm trying to remember my earliest memory of being gay. Not sure at what exact age it was, but probably right around adolescence. My earliest gay fantasies revolved around the models in the <u>International Male</u> catalogs, I began subscribing to , so that I could look at their bodies in their tight, brief, <u>very</u> form-fitting underwear! My mom had to know!?

Anyway, life was good, or so I thought? I was involved in my school classes, had many friends to do things with and seemed like your "average" all-around decent child, that I could be, being raised in that environment. That is, if you count playing Barbie's with your "girlfriends" up the street, and pretending to be a "Solid Gold" dancer in your basement, singing along to the songs!

I don't think anyone thought the wiser. Plus, our family had a little "couth" in the town, or so I thought. I was the fourth child in a line of "brainiacs" (all graduated with honors - oldest brother finished 2nd in his class, and went on to M.I.T., where my father went); brawn (both brothers were first string varsity basketball players); and beauty (sister and other brother were on both Homecoming/Prom courts, and brother was Prom King). So I think I got away with a little bit more, because of who I was. Also, my mom worked in the school district as an English teacher and substitute, as well as the ISS monitor.

So I survived high school and made it out alive. Never dated any girls (although went to most of my formal dances), and never had any sexual contact with either sex - played the virginity route. I wasn't really ready for the next phase of my life - college. I wasn't sure what I wanted to be, and maybe deep down I knew that there were some issues I needed to explore before I could go, i.e. my sexuality. But all three of my siblings went and graduated, so I was also encouraged to go, so I did; only I chose the school...

ANOM <u>AL</u> Y

Defined - peculiar, irregular, abnormal, or odd.
Seems fitting to me - they should give me a nod.
Not that I've always solely tried to be this,
When they handed out normalcy - think I was missed.

I'm attracted to those who think "outside the box"
Ones that usually don't hear the words "opportunity knocks".
We pave out our own paths, we live out our own way,
We piss many people off – we have something to say.

Liberace, Roseanne, Eminem, Lady Gaga
Mr. Manson, Mr. Warhol, Mr. Lynch, and Madonna.
They all did their own thing - they just didn't seem to care,
From their art, to their words, to their clothes that they wear.

To me being left-handed, to then knowing I'm gay,
There was no way around it - I was really born this way!
But for most of the time, I usually tried to fit in.
After trying so long, I could no longer win.

We are teachers, we're children, we're parents, and peers.
We still have the same doubts, and your issues - your fears.
It may seem that we're brave, and we don't give a shit,
If we didn't do this, we would probably quit.

We are also quite shy and at times we won't talk,
With our head usually down, as we silently walk.
We don't really like talking too much bout ourselves.
Most our thoughts and ideas lie still, lost, on our shelves.

It's so hard telling people what exactly we believe.
Easier sometimes to smile, nod, agree, and deceive.
Never know who will get us, and who will want to know more,
But to go along with them, can be such a hard chore.

As I age, I enjoy running, away from the pack.
I can only move forward, and never, ever look back.
I know I'm not alone in these words, that I say,
"I was put here on Earth, to show others the way!"

When you meet someone different, who may not be the same,
Don't dismiss that they're wrong, but remember their name.
You may never know who that anomaly is?
He or she, just might be, the great, next famous whiz!

<u>INTROVERT</u>- a shy person. Or, a person characterized by concern, primarily with his or her own thoughts and feelings.

"All this talking can hardly be said to be of any benefit to the world. It is so much waste of time. My shyness has been in reality my shield and buckler. It has allowed me to grow. It has helped me in my discernment of truth." – Gandhi

Introverted and shy can be lonely,
When we're constantly by ourselves, only.
We don't know how we got this way,
But came born with it, just like gay.
May have been helpful if someone had told me.

It's been said, we are 25% (of the pop.).
We work best under no management.
So when seeking a job,
It becomes quite a prob,
And we wonder why we even went?

At a party, I'm usually quite silent.
I use small talk as my great assignment.
Interviewing the guests,
Listening always, is best,
Then return to solitary confinement.

It's so hard being perfectly clear,
When to say what I mean is a fear.
 I'll start rambling along,
And it comes out all wrong,
Rather hand them a note and say, "Here".

But I've read that this can be a good thing.
Just imagine if no one was listening.
There'd be noise all about,
Turn our world inside out
More corruption, crime, war, in the making.

When you think you're not talking too much
Go inside yourself, breathe, get in touch
With the surroundings around you,
It's ok, do what you do,
Even when others think it's a crutch.

If you have an introverted good friend
Try some silence, sometimes, now and then.
Don't think they're being quiet,
Even you, too, can try it,
We should all take their cue, rather often.

SKEPTIC <u>AL</u>

Is that really true?
Are you sure about that?
I don't think they ever knew
What they were even looking at?

I'm not sure that I buy it.
I can't believe that it's real.
I would have to, at least, try it,
To see if it's a good deal
.

Are you serious? That's a lie!
You're not telling the truth.
Pulling the wool over my eye –
Thinking I am a sleuth.

Are you making this up?
Does that really exist?
And if that is the case,
Then that's one that I missed.

You do NOT make that much!
I'm so sure, you're THAT big???
You are SO out of touch.
That's your real hair – no wig?

You cannot be THAT old.
Are you really THAT young?
It was never THAT cold.
He cannot be THAT hung!

Now, that's probably true.
What is that, so you say?
Oh yeah, that I believe.
He is SO fuckin' gay!

EMOTION AL

Happy, Sad
Hopeful, Mad
Excited, Bored
Scared, Ignored

Anxious, Proud
Introverted, Loud
Ashamed, Reclusive
Self-loathing – abusive

Authentic, Insecure
Bold, Courageous, Demure
Self-obsessed, Isolated
Sensitive, Irritated

Conservative , Controversial
Procrastinating, Miserable
Creative, Lazy, Curious
Unconcerned, Impervious

Hopeless, Lost, Delusional
Depressed, Detached Individual
Discouraged, Vain, and Narcissistic
Moody, Numb, and Altruistic

Obsessive, Negative, Ever-weary,
Reflective, Worried Visionary.

DENI <u>AL</u>

Everything is just peachy!
Everything is just fine.
Yeah, I'm gonna finally make it.
It'll happen, anytime.

Yes, you look really good.
No, you shouldn't lose weight.
Don't forget that you could,
Show up ten minutes late.

So you work nine to five,
For an hourly wage.
That's ok, you're alive.
Doing great, for your age?

Everybody's the same.
No one's happy in life,
With their partner, or boyfriend,
Husband, lover, girlfriend, wife.

Just remember you're healthy.
You can get up each day.
People always accept you.
"Fucking faggots, go away!"

"Someday we will all be equal."
"Someday we will all be the same."

Just keep telling yourself that,
It's a no win, losing game.

Keep your head in the present.
Keep your eye on the ball.
You'll get there in your own time,
It's ok, if you crawl.

'Cause tomorrow's not now,
You can waste all today,
Sitting around, being lazy;
You've come this far, this way?

What are you really afraid of?
What's your one biggest fear?
That no one ever will like it?
Well then, why are you here?

No one waits 'til it's perfect,
'Cause it never will be.
Take the first step, and focus,
You'll be surprised what you see.

I NEVER WANTED TO BE GAY...PT. 4

And since I HAD to go to, I chose it. And boy did I ever! West Virginia University - ranked #1 party school by <u>Playboy</u> magazine, in the late '80's (this was 1987). Not the particular reason I chose this school, but it sounded like it would be fun, and I had heard it was easy to get into (seeing as my SAT scores were not that up to par). So I got in, and I partied, and partied, and partied, and repressed my sexuality, by covering it up with a borderline alcohol/drug addiction problem. I even joined a fraternity to cover up my sexuality even more, and some of my brothers thought that I may have had "alcohol poisoning" at certain times, and nicknamed me "too drunk to fuck"!

I was a mess. I thought that maybe if I did the whole "straight frat thing", that my homosexuality would go away. <u>NOT!</u> Something that is that crucially a part of you (even though, a small part), cannot really be ignored, unless you want to live in a state of denial and depression your whole life, while still sleeping with women (I don't know how men do that), eventually to screw around with a man one night and end up ruining everyone else's life, in the process (your wife's, children's, etc.).

I mean I understand the appeal of trying to live a normal hetero path "what-we-think-we-are-supposed-to-do-structured" life, but that isn't living your truth. Nowadays, it does seem a little bit more possible for men and women to be more honest with who they are, and not have to go this route. Especially since homosexuality is so "popular" now and in the mainstream of our culture (see 2005 Academy Awards (year of Brokeback Mountain) - homosexuality was everywhere).

It didn't really help me, back then, though. So I hid. I even turned my back on my best friend at one point because he came out to me. I thought he was trying to get me to come out, as well. I was so upset at him, at the time, at myself, for that, that I cut off all correspondence from him, for a couple of years. I'm so thankful now that he didn't cut me out of his life forever, because I now know that I did and do need him in my life. I realize that he wasn't trying to get me to come out. He was just sharing with me what had been going on in his.

SO...after four and a half years of abstinence and lies, and plenty of alcohol blackouts/pass outs, I was "whisked off" to a third life - the "after college world"...

2015/2023?

Another New Year,
Still am lost and in fear,
Of the fact that I'm here,
And to make it all clear?

Another Facebook post,
To brag and to boast.
It's "likes" we want most,
As our own on line host.

Another new week,
Still am trying to seek,
That while perfectly meek,
I may no longer peak.

Another endless night,
Alone and a fright.
I've lost sense of my fight,
In ever finding "Mr. Right"?

Another text sent,
It was written and went.
Sometimes hard is to vent,
And to know what is meant?

Another email read,
All verbal now dead.
What's better unsaid,
Is typed from our head.

Another new day,
And yes, I'm still gay.
I'm finding it gray,
To follow my way.

FUCK UP!

A "Fuck Up" is someone who fucks up their life,
Who cheats on their wife,
Who uses a knife,
To backstab his friends,
And makes no amends.
Who loses his job,
And lives like a slob.
Who does lots of drugs,
And refuses all hugs.
Who digs many holes,
To bury his goals.
Who's unmotivated,
And heavily sedated.
Who lets people down,
While he's sleeping around.
Who whines like a baby,
And always answers, "maybe".
A "Fuck Up" is someone who fucked up their life,
And uses a knife,
To slit both his wrists,
And knows he won't be missed.

RECESSION

Recession, Depression,
Leads to so much oppression.
Unemployed, Unenjoyed,
Is so hard to avoid.

How'd it happen? Do we know?
Will we ever start to grow?
Times are tough, life is rough,
But it's all just really "stuff".

If we hang on to hope,
We'll be able to cope.
Keep both hands firmly gripped,
Tightly secure to your rope.

I know it's easier, said than done,
Especially when, you have someone,
Who needs you now, to work, somehow,
Your offspring, your kids, your daughter, your son.

Our children will play,
Throughout all the day.
If only we could,
Try to practice their way.

To let it all go,
Not let anyone know,

Think only this thought -
"I will not let it show."

We won't alarm,
Keep them from harm,
And hope they don't see,
Through all our false charm.

But what if we fail?
And we never prevail?
Just what will become,
Of our latest sad tale?

I hope to think,
That we can't sink,
Not anymore,
Under this shore.

We'll grab a line,
Come up just fine,
And loosen our bind,
By pouring some wine.

So let us all pray,
There will finally come a day,
Confidently we will say,
"Ya know, it's gonna be ok."

DYSTHYMIA

Called a low-grade depression,
That can feel like possession,
Over all of your mind.
All good days, left behind.

Like a constant mild funk,
With some added, extra junk,
From a time long ago,
When you stopped letting go.

It takes over your life,
And could lead to some strife,
That can cause you to say,
"I don't care", "That's ok".

Never feeling that great;
You don't love – you don't hate.
But you move right along,
Not too sure, you belong.

So you try to get help,
Through the seaweed and kelp,
But you're stuck by resistance,
Drowns you slowly – no assistance.

You try pain pills and meds;
Psychotherapists shake their heads.
Have to fend for yourself,
Stay still, dusty, on that shelf.

Never forward, never back;
Yet you stay on your track,
Mediocre life will be,
All you'll ever really see.

Still you hope and you pray,
There may soon come a day,
Cause you're not <u>REALLY</u> sad,
But you're not <u>REALLY</u> glad?

You get some joy from life,
At that job, home, or wife.
And that's all that you know,
If accepted, you'll grow?

Maybe, sometime we'll see,
This is you – this is me.
"Can you live like this way?"
"Have no choice", what I'll say.

BECAUSE I'M GAY

Because I'm Gay
I ran away,
And could not stay
Another day.
Because I'm Gay
I have to say,
"That we're not weird -
We're all ok."
And I can't help
That I am gay.
I did not choose -
Was born this way.
I got to see
Because I'm Gay,
That there's not just
Only one way.
I got to play
Another day,
While finding love
In my own way.
And who's to say
That we will pay,
For all our sins,
When passed away.
I'm still like you,
I hope and pray,
That there may be
A better day.

I don't judge you
By what you say,
So why hate us,
Because we're gay.
How does what I do,
Affect you, anyway?
Or are you sad,
Life didn't go your way?
So now you waste
Another day,
Making others feel
They're not ok.
And do you think
we'll run away?
That more of us
Won't come your way?
What is so wrong
With being gay?
I do not know,
I cannot say.
But feeling hatred
Come your way,
It's hard to feel
Like I'm ok.
Let all the pain
Got in my way,
And shot myself
<u>Because I'm Gay.</u>

I NEVER WANTED TO BE GAY...PT. 5

I decided that I really wanted to move out of my hometown in PA, for a couple of reasons, but mostly, I think, subconsciously, that I would never be able to have the kind of lifestyle I thought I should have, if I chose to stay there; meaning I would've stayed in the closet.

I ended up going to Orlando, FL, because I had a friend down there from my hometown, who also knew that she needed to move away, to have the kind of lifestyle she wanted. I stayed with my friend until she connected me with a friend of hers who needed a roommate, and then I moved in with that woman. She was great. She was fun. We had some good times, as roommates go, but I was still closeted and did not feel comfortable coming out...yet.

I was waiting tables until I really decided what I wanted to do (still not really sure, but closer), and eventually started hanging out with friends from the restaurant. One night we ended up at this alternative club that had a "Bad Disco" theme on Thursdays, which was also, to my surprise, an underlying meaning for "gay night".

I started noticing that there seemed to be many more males here than females, and that's when it occurred to me, where I was. This was my first taste of what a gay bar was to feel like. And that first time we went there, I decided I would stay a little bit longer, and told my friends to leave without me.

<u>It was wild</u> - seeing men - seeing men looking at other men; men kissing, touching, groping, carousing, cruising, and even I

was finally getting "noticed", for the first time. I'm sure I was noticed prior to this, by women, but it didn't seem as "special" as what it was like to be "cruised" by other gay men. I felt wanted, finally, and it was nice to want some of them back, equally. I could finally reciprocate what I had been holding back and looking for, for so long. The moment of coming out was going to be soon!

Instantly, I started going back week after week alone, and usually ended up going home with someone else (not right off the bat, but eventually, as I became more comfortable about what I was doing). Since I didn't know any other gay men, I thought it might be nice to meet a "partner in crime" to peruse the bars with.

Well, it's kind of hard to meet another gay man to JUST be your friend, at a gay bar. Most people there, when approached, think that you are interested in them for more than "just friends" (and vice-versa), so normally that won't work. I've tried to form "friendships" with gay men in my life throughout, and a lot of the time I got burned, because they eventually thought that it was going to lead to something more, or at least something else.

Maybe I wasn't quite upfront about what I wanted as well, right away...

WE COME TO LIE (OR WE LIE TO CUM)

We come into a bar and lie to each other,
So that we can go home, and lie next to one another.
We make up false names, false places,
What we do, why we're here?
What's the point? We're all human.
Why can't we tell the truth? We're all queer.
We make small talk and tell false stories.
We compliment - "Love your hair, smile, face - tell me more please!"
We leave together, following one another home.
So much fun being a cock tease.
Why do we do it?
Is it really this fun?
When it's finally all over,
Aren't we glad it's all done?
As we're lying in bed,
We think, "when can I leave?"
Many thoughts in our head.
Was it worth it, to deceive?
As we finally get up
To crawl out of this mess,
We lie even some more -
"Here's my number, and address".
Never hear from that person, but it's fun while it lasts.
So we'll lie again next week. It's a phase we must pass.

IN A RUT

In a rut, for some butt,
At my hut. I'm a slut.

I can pass, to smoke grass,
But not on, a piece of ass.

You could offer me beer,
Which I really do dear,

But you offer me rear,
And the choice is so clear.

Love to fuck it, suck it,
Squeeze it, tease it,

Grab it, slap it,
Gotta have it!

Soft or hard, black or white,
Hairy, smooth – day or night!

Clean or dirty; wet or dry,
Muscular bubble – "My, OH MY!"

In and out, push and pull,
Feel my load, getting full.

God this feels, so damn good.
It's no wonder – as it should!

Getting close, gonna explode,
Holy shit! Shot my load!

WHORE!

I'M A WHORE!
Want some more.
Out the door,
'Til I'm sore.
It's a chore,
Not a bore,
Home by four,
When a whore.

I'M A SLUT!
Not some nut,
Who's uncut,
Or stuck up.
In a rut,
For some butt,
At my hut,
When a slut.

I'M A SLEAZE!
And a tease.
Spend my time,
On my knees.
Never worry,
About disease.
"Oh god, Please!"
When a sleaze.

I'M A TRAMP!
With a cramp,
From my legs,
In a clamp.
Now my sheets
Are all damp,
And I'm spent
'Cause a tramp.

I'm a person.

ADULTERY

The night falls.
Two sets of eyes gaze at each other, from across the room.

The seduction begins.
The exchange of names and numbers is offered.
The invitation to the other's home.

The seduction deepens.
Soft caresses and touches across each other's bodies.
The hard sculptured muscles felt under each other's clothes.
The light kisses on the lips,
The exchange and intertwining of each other's tongues.
Hands move slowly under the clothes to touch the warm skin.
Clothes are removed.

The seduction is in full motion.
The deep, hard, wet kisses.
The grinding motion of each other's bodies pressed against each other.
Moans and lovemaking sounds are heard throughout the room,
Hands stroke every part of each other's nakedness.
Mad, passionate heat is rising from every inch of each other's bodies.
The eruption of orgasms explodes to a silent halt.

The seduction ends.

The drive home to the husband.

I FEEL SORRY FOR YOU

"I feel sorry for you, because of the way you look."
Your fat, out-of-proportion-like figure you call a body

"I feel sorry for you, because of what you do."
You work at a video store for some chump change amount of money, when you have a degree from a university

"I feel sorry for you, because of how you live."
In a sloppy two-bedroom apartment, with a roommate, in the worst part of town, with clutter all over – you're a disgrace

"I feel sorry for your family."
You let them down, when you moved from your hometown and started your "secret life", and never bothered to let any of them into it

"I feel sorry for your friends."
You never tell them how you really feel, or what you're thinking – you're a coward and a phony

"I really feel sorry for you."

And then I walked away from the mirror.

NOTHING, SEEMS TO WORK FOR ME.

So at the age of 53, some might say that I haven't done a god damn thing with my life?

Does earning a bachelor's degree in 4.5 years, directly after high school, sound like <u>nothing</u>?

Does moving to Orlando, FL, from a small-town in PA, w/o a job, and knowing only one other person down there, sound like <u>nothing</u>?

Does dealing with my sexuality and "coming out", to all my family and friends, sound like <u>nothing</u>?

Does driving across country to live in San Francisco sound like <u>nothing</u>?

Does moving to LA w/o knowing a single soul, to fulfill my "dreams" of doing something creative, and maybe in the entertainment industry, sound like <u>nothing</u>?

Does moving in with a partner out to the desert, to start and build a new life together, sound like <u>nothing</u>?

Does consistently working on my creative craft, in abstract art; and trying to get those expressions out into the world, to share w/others, sound like <u>nothing</u>?

Well, **<u>nothing</u>** seems to work well for me. I may not be the ideal "picture" of what society has taught us to be, but I may be on my way, and even if I'm not, who cares?

Because along the way, I've gotten to see different places, explore different lifestyles, meet different people, make different friends, and take different challenges?

I've also had to sacrifice many things along my way – holidays/vacations, away from family and friends; stability in owning a home and starting a family; and my own sanity, in feelings of lost, loneliness, and depression, in trying to figure out what life is all about.

And who's to say that my way is the right way? I won't tell anyone that. I spend most of my time wishing I could get to the point where everyone else is, or seems, but I guess I'm just not ready, and that's ok.

Because if I think about it, if I'd already known what I'd wanted to do, and what I wanted out of life, directly after college, I may already be bored with that.

This way it's been interesting, and quite a "struggle" at times, but I'm slowly finding out who I am and where I belong. Maybe none of us really belong in any particular place. It's just where we end up that seems like where we're supposed to be.

I think any of us could fit in and belong anywhere at all, and that's what makes life so great. We can do anything we want, and no one can tell us if it's right or wrong – **<u>you just know it's for you!</u>**

I NEVER WANTED TO BE GAY...PT. 6

It's interesting - when you're ready to "come out" and enjoy the whole process of gay bars and the community. I'm not sure how most gay men do it, if they're by themselves. I guess unless you grow up in a big city mecca where gay men are more prevalent, and you already have some friends there who are also gay, well, then, you're lucky. If you're like me and come from small-town, "middle-of-nowhere-America", and you NEED to move away in order to "come out"; and you're also afraid to ask any of your coworkers if they're gay or not; and you're "posing" as someone who is not gay (even though you're not really trying - you're just being yourself), well, then, you'll have to do it on your own!

<u>And I did.</u> And then I thought I would be able to meet a bunch of new gay friends by "hanging out" in the bars/clubs. Well, that was a disappointment, because everybody already has enough friends, and they're only hoping to go home with you and get off. This can be quite discouraging. No wonder so many men never come out.

So, you do the whole mess-around-with-one-guy-and-start-to-see-him-out-more-and-more-and-eventually-become-hangout-buddies-thing for a while, just so you don't seem to be so much of a loner. Hoping that one day you will finally be able to tell the other gay men who continue to approach you, that you're really not interested in them in that way, but maybe we can be "friends"? <u>NOT!</u>

That's a disadvantage of being a "people pleaser" (me) - sometimes you tend to get yourself in some potentially risky situations, and do things/guys that you normally wouldn't do, but you don't want to let the other people down, so you just let yourself down. How many times have I got off with someone, so as to not make that other person feel undesirable or pathetic, or just so I can get out of a situation faster, after you both cum?

<u>I'm not very proud of myself this way.</u> This can't be how heterosexuals do it, is it? I'm sure for some of them it is. Since I really didn't know what to do, and no one gave me a map of what I was "supposed" to do, or any sort of structure or "game plan", as heterosexuals seem to have, what did I care what I did, or tried, or caught, or lied about? No one had taught me what homosexuals were supposed to do, society and historically wise, so I guess I sort of felt like I was on my own to cum up with that (literally).

So I did what I thought I was "supposed" to do as a gay man, from learning through my peers, my vision, and the media, and it didn't always seem like a "road that I needed to be on", and sometimes felt as if I was really just trying to get off that road, if you know what I mean. There were plenty of things I did in Orlando that I was ashamed of, but maybe that was me just not letting myself have my truths. Or they really were my truths, and I couldn't just let myself feel ok about them?

I think part of me thought that this was the way that gay men lived. Another part of me didn't like that, even though I continued to do it <u>over and over and over again.</u>

Maybe it was different for me, because I was dealing with my homosexuality for the first time, head on, AND I was also trying to figure out what I wanted to do with my life - work/career-wise. I have to think that part of me felt so much anger and despair around the fact that I was gay, and that I had to get through this life, being gay; that I maybe, subconsciously, sabotaged whatever sort of "career goals" I had, and said "fuck it".

I guess I may have felt that if somebody wasn't going to show me the way that I am "supposed" to live my life (as I felt hetero's had been given), then I was just going to do whatever the hell I wanted to, and not worry about it. I mean, the way I felt like I saw how homosexuals were viewed was, well, if they don't really want to think of us (our type) as being up to par with the rest of the country, i.e. equal rights, then why the hell should I care about myself?

GAY CLICHÉ

You drive your SUV, down the boulevard,

Cell phone up to your ear, think you're some kind of star.

Spend most of your time, in the gym working out,

'Cause you're really insecure, and you have lots of doubt.

Chorus - (You're such a) Gay Cliché!

(You work it) Everyday!

(You're just a) Gay Cliché!

(You choose to see it) No other way!

You're always out in the club, taking god knows what.

Your jeans are so damn tight, so they can show off your butt.

You Tivo "Will and Grace" and "Queer as Folk".

When you gonna wake up, and learn your life is a joke.

Chorus – (You're such a) Gay Cliché!

(You sleep with) Men who pay!

(You're just a) Gay Cliché!

(Your porn star status) Expired today

Bridge – You spend all day long, trying to make yourself hot,

so you can strut your tired self thru the city.

But when you finally realize that it's not what got,

or how you look, you're gonna feel mighty shitty.

You shave and wax your hairs, from your body now,

And don't forget to trim your bush, and pluck your one eyebrow.

Do you think that anyone care's that you are so damn hot?

There's a million others out there like you, you are somebody not!

Repeat second chorus, then first chorus

"You work it!"

SEROCONVERSION

I thought I always played it so safe,
But now I find myself feeling hate,
In wondering how I went wrong,
So now I sing you this song,
And realize that this time, it's too late.

You taught me always to love myself.
I put that love tucked away, on a shelf,
And gave myself to some more,
Because I wanted to score,
And wanted someone to love me as well.

Chorus : **I spent two weeks waiting in hell,**
To find out that I'm not doing well,
And what I'm trying to say,
Is I'm in a bad way.
I'm calling you, cause I know you won't tell.

I hope your judgment of me, will soon pass.
I never tried crystal meth, or smoked grass.
Just wanted only some fun,
Didn't want to hurt anyone,
But now it's come to a point I can't pass.

It's really sad that some people won't say,
If they're infected before they just play.
You ask if they're positive,
They say, "No, they'd rather live",
When they don't really know their status.

<u>**Chorus**</u>

<u>Bridge :</u> I never thought that this could happen to me.
It's time I woke myself up, and started to see,
That nothing good can come from getting H-I-V!

<u>**Chorus**</u> **: (change the last line)**
I called you up, so I hope you won't tell.

OVER YOU

I'm all alone,
Out on my own,
Away from home,
And you're not coming to the phone.

You little prick,
Can suck my dick,
Next time you think you can bring
Another guy home to trick.

Chorus: **And I'm so glad I got over you!**
I'm really happy now I know that we're through.
And if you think I'll ever want you back in my life,
Well, all I have to say is, "Ah, boo-hoo!"

All by myself,
With no one else,
Down here in hell,
And hoping you're not doing well.

You fucking whore.
You'll soon get yours
I hope you're sore,
When that guy throws you out the door!

Chorus

Music interlude

Repeat chorus

(slower and softer)
It's really true.

We're really through.
I'm black and blue,
From all my happiness, over you.

DESPAIR

<u>Chorus</u> – Walking down the road to nowhere
Living my life without a care
Hanging my head, in despair
Hoping I'll soon see you up there
Walking down the road to nowhere
Breathing in dirty, dusty air
Wondering if I'll see you this year
Wishing to end all of my fear

Just out of school, without a job
Messing my life up, just like a slob.
Feeling depressed – feeling alone.
Miles away from my last happy home.
Taking the time to sing you this song.
Don't know how I could have really gone wrong?
Hopefully soon, I will see you again.
Where will it be? Where have I been?

<u>**Chorus**</u>

Got up this morning, talked to myself.
Praying that I'm still in really good health.
Found a few coins, along the way,
Maybe they won't make me pay them today.
Where am I going? What can I do?
All I can think of is being with you
Is this really all that life is about?
Or is staying alive, really a doubt?

<u>**Chorus**</u>

It's time to go, I soon see the end.
I see someone, coming around the bend.
I gave it a try, but it's too hard to play.
This game on this road is now fading away.
I just hope you will do better than me.
Just don't lose your dreams, because that is the key.
Please never forget me, whatever you do.
I will always be silently walking with you.

SUICID <u>AL</u>

Swallow pills, razorblades, or a gun?
When did life become not very fun?
Even though I will probably be missed,
And I'm sure some may even be pissed.
But I've had a good time up 'til now.
There's sometimes when I wonder, still how?
Self-medicating with pot, booze, and food,
Gets you through, matters not, what your mood.
Should I leave a long note or a letter?
Or just say that, "It never got better!"
I realize that someone has to find me.
I apologize for how hard that could be.
People should not be sad and not crying,
Over my selfishness and my dying.
I was happy for awhile, but I no longer smile,
And I find myself constantly sighing.
So I guess I should choose when and where,
And the time of the day – do I care?
Or is this, just maybe, too extraneous?
Do you think others are more spontaneous?
If I don't want to make a big mess,
I suppose popping pills will be best.
Just to fall fast asleep, in the vastness, so deep,
My soul, hopefully, to always be blessed.
Maybe all of us feel this each day.
"If I can just get through", is the real way.
'Cause it's all gonna end - all in time, my good friend,
Just remember, tomorrow's not today.

I NEVER WANTED TO BE GAY...PT. 7

I lived it up for about 5 years in Orlando, having anonymous sex, anonymous drugs, and a lot of anonymous misunderstandings with myself, in how or what I thought living the gay lifestyle was supposed to be. I did finally acquire some gay friends, but they were mostly from the "bar scene", and didn't play any other sort of relevance in my life. OR, they were guys I "dated" for awhile until it ended, and at that point, they usually didn't want anything more to do with me.

I did manage to "hang" with one guy for about four years, in Orlando. He, I would have to say, played an intricate part on my formative homosexual years, and helped me to establish a little bit more clarity in my thinking of who I wanted to be/am today. Of course, he was eight years older than me, and maybe I felt a little "safe" with that type of "father figure" in my life, as he took me under his wing, and made everything ok, <u>when it wasn't.</u>

He wasn't really "out" yet, either, at least to his coworkers - he didn't really have any other friends. I can't help but think I fall for or go for these types of guys who generally aren't in the "thick of things", as far as the gay community went. They were usually very "straight-acting"/masculine, and most of the time, they were "perceived" as being heterosexual amongst their peers. I think that there probably was/is some underlying meaning for me, in going for that type of man, and has a lot to do with some of my own insecurities around being gay, and how I wanted to be "perceived" as well. We call this "internalized homophobia", and it runs rampant in our community, more so than any other community out there.

I've had many a thought(s) around this issue, and am closer and closer to finally being ok with who I am, and more importantly, who or how I see myself as a gay man. I am realizing more and more each day that it doesn't "define" who I am, which I think I thought did, in the past. Now I see more clearly what I want/don't want, as far as how much of my life I do want to make be about my sexuality, and am trying to create my own way, as far as what I would like to think of as the way I can live my life, be it gay or straight. I'm starting to now see the value in not having a learned/perceived "structure" given to me throughout those formative years, because now I feel I can choose whatever path I'd like to take, and it will always be the right path, because it is mine.

Even though, I thought doing whatever I wanted to wasn't good for me, in Orlando, it was due to the things I was doing, that I didn't feel were good for me. Now, I'm consciously choosing things that I know work for me, and that will fill my life with more positivity and enrichment, so I can feel good about the choices I make.

AWAKE

As I lie here awake,
Before dawn nearly breaks,
I am saddened by thoughts of my past.

Of my family, my friends;
Wondering how it all ends,
Realizing, it goes by so fast.

Do you think we can see,
When we turn thirty-three,
Fifty-four (current age), just how life's gonna be?

Always thought that was old.
At least, seemed, when was told,
Growing up, slowly, at seventeen.

It's like I'm already half done,
And really – what have I become?
Single, unemployed – is this it for me?

Is this how it's supposed to go?
Do we really even know?
But we keep moving on, steadily.

We all take what were given,
And try to make it our living -
Is that really such a bad place to be?

I want the people that knew,
All the things I've been through,
That I hope never caused much worry.

Never imagined the day,
When I found out, "I'm gay".
How I turned it into such tragedy.

Wanted always to be something;
Thought I never was special.
Was that life, teaching me, irony?

It had singled me out,
Which created more doubt,
In myself, and my own humanity.

I had let so many years,
Fly by in shame, and many tears,
When I should have seen, how I was lucky!

Isolated myself,
Put my dreams on a shelf,
Let them gather dust, waiting for me.

So the moral I'm told,
Is you're never too old,
To do what you want, creatively.

Is where I'm at, for tomorrow,
It could end all in sorrow.
I could be gone. Eternity.

HOPE

When our president's motto,
Can be so hard to follow.
Someone says to you, "Nope".
That's your time to gain Hope.

Often hard to believe,
Harder yet, to receive,
But without it we're lost,
Usually at a high cost.

Just a simple four letters
Can make everyone better.
Needs and wants never met
But with Hope you can get.

Faith is good, love is grand,
Hope will always lend a hand.
When it's just out of reach,
It will rescue, and teach.

You may be destitute,
Or just down on your luck.
If you always have this,
Things may no longer suck.

We all have a bad day,
When we're stuck in our head.
And we think we might be,
Maybe, better off dead?

Tell yourself this won't last
Just let go of your rope.
Take a breath, look around,
And remember there's Hope.

Hope for joy, Hope for pain,
For the sun and the rain.
At the times we're in strife,
Hope will be there, for life.

No matter where, when, or how,
It will show up somehow.
You no longer will mope.
Once you see, you have Hope.

WOUNDED HEALER

Wounded Healer, kindred souls,
Born apart, to fill your holes.
Have no say – we're born this way,
Here to teach, yet learn to pray.
We understand, it makes no sense.
We'd like to be on your side of the fence.
I may not believe it, if just one or two,
But when thousands come out, I'd think it was true.
We have no agenda; not here to convert.
We just want to live, as you do, without hurt.
Can you not see it from our point of views?
Just put yourself, one time, alone, in our shoes.
You accepted the Jews, and accepted the blacks.
So why is it we can't still slip through those cracks?
We don't spend time thinking about you and your life.
So stop thinking of ours and you'll end all our strife.
We are flattered that you think about us so much.
We feel sorry for you. You are so out of touch.
It's really a shame; it's inevitable,
We'll eventually be equal, same, and humanely full.
We want to assist you; we know how you feel,
There's no easy way to get through your ordeal.
We're here to tell you that all is ok.
It's ok if you're different – it's ok if you're gay.

SLEEP

I'm deprived of my sleep,
So I start to count sheep.
The more I toss and turn,
Seems like there's more to learn,

About relaxing my mind,
And leaving worry behind.
It happens time and again,
Like my thoughts always win.

I wonder why ; I scream "No!"
That never works – they won't go.
It's like I'm doomed; somehow I'm bad.
I know the answer, because I'm sad.

I lie awake and ponder more.
My mind keeps racing – getting sore.
The daylight's coming – it's morning soon.
Say hello to the sun, and good-bye to the moon.

I'll be so freaking tired; I'll know I'll have to cope,
But it matters not much, when all I do is just mope.
The day will crawl and I will weep,
'Til night returns, and I try to sleep.

ANOTHER DAY, ANOTHER PITY; ANOTHER GAY IN, YET, ANOTHER CITY!

Why is it that the gays move so many times, to soooo many different cities? I've talked to numbers of them, and we've all lived in Miami, New York, Los Angeles, San Francisco; and now, for me, Palm Springs! And since I've moved here (a year ago,) I've already run into some of the same gays I used to hang out with, when we both lived in a previous city. The gays like to change their cities, like their latest new club/bar.

At 44, this is my fourth big city move. I've moved from Orlando, Fl. (after college in West Virginia; after graduating high school in PA), to San Francisco, to Los Angeles, to San Diego, back to Los Angeles, and now to Palm Springs. What is it we're looking for? What are we running from? Or are we all just a little bit too bored, too often?

For me, I think it's always been a combination of all of the above. First off, as an artist, I already have that "gypsy" mentality, of switching jobs, wondering where my next meal will come from, and always feeling "unsettled". So I never really felt grounded or secure enough anywhere, because of my "profession". Now had I been discovered early on as a great artiste, been given my own gallery and studio to work in, and was making a living at it, I may have not moved. That was not the case. But that's my excuse. <u>What's everyone else's?</u>

The men I've encountered that have done this have told me everything from transferring for a job, to moving for a man, breaking up with a man, and just feeling it was time. All are good and valid reasons to do so. Maybe it's just in our genes. It may not be such a bad thing to have in our genetic makeup? Besides the fact that it's a bitch to pack up, sell, or throw away all our crap, each and every time we make this transition, it always turns into a greater thing later. Because really, what are we missing, from staying?

I think each and every one of us (gay or straight) can be comfortable and find some enjoyment in any environment we go to; and of course as gay men, we do have to thrive towards the bigger cities, in order to find some sort of like-minded community, which we can enmesh our lives in. So, instead of looking at it, as if it's "weird, odd, or unusual", I think we should embrace the fact that we do, and can rightly so. I mean, for most of us, we'll probably not get married, have children, or even own a home, so why not?

It may make us seem "flighty", or noncommittal to anything, or any person, but so what? It's our life, right? Plus we get to see and live in some of the greatest cities in the world. We get to experience new places, new restaurants, new people, lifestyles, and environments. Not everyone will get that luxury to do that in their life. And some of us will never even leave our towns in which we grew up in. And that's ok, too. Everyone's entitled and given their choices in life, and how they want to lead them. I do understand, also, some of us will not be able to move, for financial or health reasons, and I'm sorry for those in situations as this, that want to move. I am ever grateful I've been blessed with good health and finances.

I'd love to know what the gays in other countries do – whether or not they also move from city to city, looking for the "next best thing"? Especially those living in countries where same sex marriage IS legal?

And what will really happen to us, once we are equal counterparts on all levels with our heterosexual brothers and sisters? Will there be a "shift" in our thought process, because we will be getting married more, having families, and putting down roots permanently where we are?

Equality is really just right around the corner, and with that comes a price? Will the ever single, party-boy, transient lifestyle become obsolete? Will we then succumb to what we've thought we've always wanted, which was to be just like "them"? Or is this really just about personality type, more than sexuality type? Maybe it's just me, and my other fellow "gypsies", who I seem to keep encountering? Maybe it's not a gay man thing after all? Maybe it's just a choice some of us make? - 2013

I NEVER WANTED TO BE GAY...PT. 8

After leaving Orlando, I finally came clean to most everybody, about who I was, including roommate(s), coworkers, family members, and close friends. There were still a "select" few who did not know my secret, but I'm sure it wasn't too hard for them to figure out. Everyone's reaction was positive, accepting, felt safe, and not at all judgmental. I think the one person who may have had the biggest problem with this "awakening", was my mother, who funnily enough, was the one who prompted me to come out...

We were making a road trip back to North East, from Orlando, and had about 15 hours to kill. I had decided ahead of time that this would be the moment I would "disclose" my sexuality to her. Somehow, homosexuality came up (?) - I think it may have had to do with the conference she was just at, in Tampa, but not really sure - and I really wasn't too sure how I would start the conversation, so this prompted me.

She asked, "Oh, is that a pink triangle (referring to my red hazard button, which glows pink when the car lights are on)?" I said, "No, but since you brought it up, do you know what it means?" She replied with a yes or something like that, and I said, "Well, since you brought it up, I should let you know that I am gay." And the first words from her mouth were, "Are you sure?"

I took this as a cue that she may have had a problem with this, so then we talked about everything regarding the issue - which friends of mine I thought were also gay (or already knew), when I first knew, what I knew about the lifestyle, and her disappointment in that I may never get to be a father. I also asked her to not "out" me to any other family members, but she did anyhow, and my father's reaction was, "I already knew that."

It's interesting to me to know that my father already knew, but my mother "seemed" surprised. I thought it would have been the other way around. I also thought that they would have already discussed this together. I guess, I just thought that's what parents do. Maybe he felt that if he said anything to my Mom, she would start worrying, and he wanted to spare her concerns/feelings, until he actually could confirm it.

So...the family knew, the friends knew, the coworkers knew. Everyone "seemed" fine with it. **<u>Except myself.</u>** ☹ I still didn't like knowing that I would have to continue disclosing this to people throughout my life (not that I had to), or even worse, that they could already tell I was gay. I also think that a lot of this had to stem around the fact that I still wasn't sure what I wanted to do with my life, and somehow, in some way, I think that I thought my sexuality was holding me back.

But now I had no more excuses. I told everyone, everyone was cool with it, and I still felt the same way about life in general - that it was still going to be incredibly hard, and that I may never feel content with where I'm at. I think I thought that I might get a bad/negative reaction from somebody (not really) I would tell, and then I could use that as my excuse for not feeling so good about myself and my life, but that never happened. Thus began another stage...

I moved back from Orlando to North East, PA (that's right, you heard right). My roommate had moved out and went back to

Ohio, and I wasn't ready to get another "stranger" in there for a roommate, plus I was unhappy with my current position with Blockbuster - hey, I gave them four good years of work, from me. It was time to make a clean break...(12/1998)

Al Walz currently resides in Palm Springs, CA, where, to this day, he still doesn't think he's any closer to figuring out what he wants to do with his life? He's still an artist, in many capacities (writing, visual, singing), but now knows that probably no one ever figures out what they want to do? They just fall into things, choose different things, get jobs, quit jobs, start a family, get a divorce...there's no right or wrong path or direction. Just live, because at the end of the day, at the end of your life, that's the only thing that's going to matter. That **YOU LIVED!**

AL WALZ shares thoughts, poems, and free-form essays in his autobiographical journey of his coming out process, and accepting his sexuality. Hoping to connect with others who also were/are conflicted, thinking he'd be always considered a minority, he found his own way to deal with this new information, knowing each of us will also meander at our own pace, during this period. He taps into his aggression, anger, sadness, hopelessness, and strength with humor, wit, sarcasm, and creative expression (poetry, diatribes, stories) of his own life experiences, which helped him stay sane, positive, hopeful, and optimistic. His views may be outdated (from 1992-98), and shouldn't be taken out of context. He knows how troublesome it can be for one to come to terms with something that feels like it may detour your life, send you in a downward spiral, and have you thinking you may never be happy, content, or joyful with day to day existing.

In 2023, he thinks our world has come closer to being onboard with the idea that being gay is not a choice, and doesn't define who you are. It's one aspect of our being, and honestly, sometimes, now, he feels like it's been a blessing (not a curse). "It's opened myself up to accepting and embracing other marginalized groups, sharing in the "big picture" that we're all just humans, trying to cohabit ate freely and openly, while we're on this planet, for just our own brief time."

Al still resides in southern California, where he continues to work on exploring and expanding his artistic endeavors – visual, abstract, mixed-media pieces; singing, and writing.